DEC 1 0 ...

D0643641

Rita Santos

CAMILA CABELLO

CUBAN AMERICAN SINGER

creative Having the ability to create new things.

culture The beliefs and customs of a place or people.

degree A title given by a school to show that a student has completed a course of study.

desperate Needing something badly.

determined Believing in and working toward a goal.

heritage The shared traditions and history of a group of people.

immigrate To move to a new country.

infrastructure The basic equipment and buildings of a town or larger area.

inspired Moved to do something.

Contents

Words to Know 2

Chapter 1 Leaving Home 5

Chapter 2 Fighting Their Fears 8

Chapter 3 Jumping................................14

Chapter 4 Going Her Own Way.............19

Timeline.................................22

Learn More 23

Index 24

Camila Cabello

When young Camila was growing up, her family loved to celebrate. Family gatherings were always full of singing and dancing. But Camila was shy. Sometimes she even cried if anyone asked her to sing! Still, being around music taught Camila to love it. No one knew that when she finally found her voice, the whole world would listen.

FROM HAVANA TO MEXICO

Karla Camila Cabello Estrabao was born on March 3, 1997, in Havana, Cuba. Her family always called her by her middle name. Camila's mother, Sinuhe, was from Cuba. Her father, Alejandro, was born in Mexico City, Mexico. Camila traveled a lot when she was young. Her parents wanted the best for her. They were always looking for a better life. This meant that they moved back and forth

Camila had a Taylor Swift poster in her room growing up.

between Havana and Mexico City many times. Cuba and Mexico are both Latin American countries. They have different **cultures**, but people in both countries mostly speak Spanish.

Camila spent part of her childhood here in Havana, Cuba.

STARTING OVER

Education was very important to Camila's family. Her parents wanted her to go to the best schools. They felt the United States was the best place for Camila to start school. She was six years old. She was too young to understand how nervous her parents were to immigrate to the United States. They moved to Miami, Florida. They had no friends or family there.

Camila was excited to make friends in her new school. The only problem was she hadn't learned English yet! She practice her new language by watching American cartoons. Immigration was hard, but some parts were fun!

Camila Says:

"We have home in us. Because we brought it with us."

CHAPTER 2
FIGHTING THEIR FEARS

In Havana, Camila's mother was an architect. But companies in the United States wouldn't hire her. They did not recognize her **degrees** from Cuban schools. Sinuhe had to find work placing goods on store shelves. It paid very little. Camila knew her parents struggled to make ends meet.

WORKING HARD

One day Sinuhe met another Cuban woman in Florida. The woman's brother needed an architect who knew how to use a certain computer program. **Desperate** for

Camila Says:

"Immigrants have the hunger to do the impossible."

Camila's mother, shown here, worked hard to create a better life for her family in the United States.

Camila's family settled in Miami, Florida, in 2003.

a better job, Sinuhe claimed she knew the program. She got the job. Sinuhe went home and taught herself the computer program. Through hard work and some luck Sinuhe's dream had come true. She was finally able to offer her family a better life.

Camila admired her mother's bravery and her willingness to try something new. Her mother told her about the day they came to the United States. She said, "That day, I knew if I thought about it, fear would make me turn back. That's why when you're afraid, you force yourself to jump. You don't think, you just jump."

DREAMING BIG

Camila had a dream, too. The little girl who was too shy to sing in front of her family sang whenever she was alone. She loved to sing. But her fear kept her from

Camila became a United States citizen when she was ten years old.

Camila was nervous about performing in front of a large crowd. But she overcame her fears and began her singing career when she appeared on *The X-Factor*.

letting anyone know. Camila was inspired by her mother's bravery. She decided she needed to jump, too. At fifteen, she asked her parents to let her audition for the show *The X-Factor*. On the show, singers would perform in front of famous musicians. They could help them develop their creative voice.

Camila's parents were shocked. Their shy little girl was asking for the chance to sing in front of millions of people. But Camila knew a little bravery was all she needed. Camila's beautiful voice amazed her parents and the judges. She and a few other contestants formed a group. They were called Fifth Harmony.

Part of a Band

Fifth Harmony did not win, but they finished in third place. Soon, the group was offered a record deal. Camila's parents were pleased with her success. Still, they wanted her to get a good education. Camila left Miami Palmetto

Camila Says:

"Feel the fear and do it anyway."

Camila (*far left*) and the other members of Fifth Harmony were finalists in the 2012 *X-Factor* competition.

High School to follow her dreams, but she continued her studies. Camila completed her degree while on the road.

Being part of a band was hard work. Fifth Harmony's song "Worth It," from their second album, hit number 12 on the charts. Camila loved her bandmates and the experience of making albums with them. But she found

Camila and Fifth Harmony perform at the Billboard Music Awards in 2016.

Camila sang Aretha Franklin's "Respect" at her *X-Factor* audition.

herself writing lots of songs that weren't quite right for the band. She longed for the freedom to follow her own dreams. On December 18, 2016, she announced she was leaving the band to begin her solo career.

Going Solo

Leaving the group was scary. Camila didn't know if she could make it on her own. Still, she was **determined** to try. Shortly after leaving the group, her childhood idol,

Taylor Swift, asked Camila to join her on tour. Every night, Camila would join her new friend onstage to help sing Taylor's hit "Shake It Off." Once again, a little bit of bravery went a long way in helping Camila's dreams come true.

After deciding to go solo, Camila was invited to tour with Taylor Swift.

Bravery, talent, and luck had gotten Camila where she was. But she hadn't forgotten the people who'd helped her family along the way. She knew it was important to give back.

A CHANCE TO HELP

In 2017, Hurricane Maria devastated Puerto Rico. Much of the island's infrastructure was destroyed. People were without power for months. Many people died. The American government was criticized for not sending enough help to the island.

Latino Americans felt the government was ignoring

Camila's star continued to rise in 2017. Here she performs at an awards show in London, England.

Camila was influenced by Latin American artists like Alejandro Fernández and Celia Cruz.

their community. Puerto Rican playwright Lin-Manuel Miranda wanted to help the people of the island be heard. He wrote a song called "Almost Like Praying." The song's lyrics name every town in Puerto Rico. Lin-Manuel asked Hispanic musicians from all over Latin America to be a part of the song. Camila was overjoyed when she was asked to help. The song helped raise money for victims of the hurricane.

Lin-Manuel Miranda asked Camila and other Hispanic performers to be part of a song that raised money for victims of Hurricane Maria in Puerto Rico.

GOING BACK TO HER ROOTS

Camila enjoyed being able to help others and to celebrate Latin American music. She wanted to let the world know she was proud of who she was. She decided to take a chance on her first solo album. Rather than just writing American pop songs, she allowed the music she'd heard as a child to influence her. In August 2017, Camila released the song "Havana." It was a celebration of her Cuban heritage and the city in which she was born.

In 2018, Camila took home four American Music Awards.

Once again, Camila was right to follow her heart. The song quickly became one of the most popular songs on her debut album, *Camila*. She knew that being true to herself would always bring success.

Camila Says:

"We (immigrants) aren't fearless. We just have dreams bigger than our fears."

TIMELINE

1997 Camila is born in Havana, Cuba, on March 3.

2003 Moves to Miami, Florida.

2008 Becomes a United States citizen.

2012 Auditions for television show *The X-Factor*.

2013 Fifth Harmony puts out their first EP, *Better Together*.

2015 Fifth Harmony puts out their debut album, *Reflections*.

2016 Camila leaves Fifth Harmony to start her solo career.

2017 Joins Lin-Manuel Miranda and others on the charity song "Almost Like Praying."

2018 Releases debut album, *Camila*. Wins four American Music Awards, including New Artist of the Year.

LEARN MORE

BOOKS

Lajiness, Katie. *Camila Cabello*. Minneapolis, MN: ABDO, 2018.

Moon, Walt K. *Let's Explore Cuba*. New York, NY: Lerner Classroom, 2017.

Watts, Franklin. *Fifth Harmony: The Dream Begins Now*. New York, NY: Orchard Books, 2014.

WEBSITES

Camila Cabello

Camilacabello.com

Learn about the singer's upcoming albums.

National Geographic Kids: Cuba

kids.nationalgeographic.com/explore/countries/cuba

Learn more about Cuba and other Latin American countries.

INDEX

C
Cabello, Sinuhe, 5, 8–11
Camila, 21
childhood, 5–7, 11–13
Cuba, 5–6, 8, 21

E
education, 7, 14–16

F
family, 5–6, 8–11, 14
Fifth Harmony, 14–17

G
giving back, 20–21

H
Hurricane Maria, 19–20

M
Mexico, 5–6
Miranda, Lin-Manuel, 20
moves to United States, 7, 8, 11

P
Puerto Rico, 19–20

S
solo career, 17, 21
Swift, Taylor, 17–18

X
X-Factor, The, 13, 14

Published in 2020 by Enslow Publishing, LLC.
101 W. 23rd Street, Suite 240, New York, NY 10011

Copyright © 2020 by Enslow Publishing, LLC.

Library of Congress Cataloging-in-Publication Data
Names: Santos, Rita, author.
Title: Camila Cabello : Cuban American singer / Rita Santos.
Description: New York : Enslow Publishing, [2020] | Series: Junior biographies | Audience: Grades 3-5.
  Includes bibliographical references and index.
Identifiers: LCCN 2018046710| ISBN 9781978507487 (library bound) | ISBN
  9781978508804 (pbk.) | ISBN 9781978508811 (6 pack)
Subjects: LCSH: Cabello, Camila, 1997–Juvenile literature. | Singers—United
  States—Biography—Juvenile literature. | Cubans—United States—Biography—Juvenile literature.
Classification: LCC ML3930.C16 S26 2018 | DDC 782.42164092 [B] —dc23
LC record available at https://lccn.loc.gov/2018046710

Printed in the United States of America

To Our Readers: We have done our best to make sure all website addresses in this book were active and appropriate when we went to press. However, the author and the publisher have no control over and assume no liability for the material available on those websites or on any websites they may link to. Any comments or suggestions can be sent by e-mail to customerservice@enslow.com.

Photos Credits: Cover, p. 1 Jeff Kravitz/FilmMagic, Inc./Getty Images; pp. 4, 18 John Shearer/Getty Images; p. 6 Kamira/Shutterstock.com; p. 9 Mike Coppola/WireImage/Getty Images; p. 10 Mia2you/Shutterstock.com; p. 12 Monica Schipper/FilmMagic/Getty Images; p. 15 Gregg DeGuire/WireImage/Getty Images; p. 16 Kevin Winter/Getty Images; p. 19 Tim P. Whitby/Getty Images; p. 20 Daniel Boczarski/Getty Images; p. 21 David Crotty/Patrick McMullan/Getty Images; interior page bottoms (musical notes) abstract/Shutterstock.com.